Ten-Minute Thinking Tie-Ins

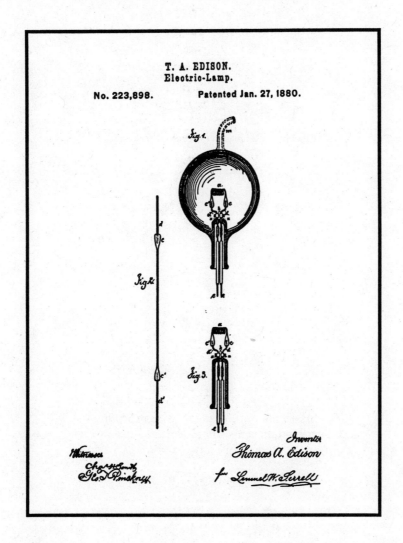

by Murray Suid and Wanda Lincoln

Illustrated by Mike Artell

This book is for Christopher Parker

Publisher: Roberta Suid
Editor: Beverly Cory
Design: David Hale
Production: Susan Pinkerton

Other books by the authors: *Book Factory,
Editing, Greeting Cards, Letter Writing,
More Book Factory, Picture Book Factory,
Report Factory, Research, Sentences,
Stories, Write Through the Year, Writing Hangups.*

Entire contents copyright ©1992 by Monday Morning
Books, Inc., Box 1680, Palo Alto, California 94302

Monday Morning is a registered trademark of
Monday Morning Books, Inc.

ISBN 1-878279-39-4

Printed in the United States of America
9 8 7 6 5 4 3 2 1

For a complete catalog, write to the address above.

CONTENTS

INTRODUCTION

People who want to get physically fit don't just work on their biceps. They give attention to all their muscles.

Likewise, those teachers who want to help students become better thinkers provide a program that awakens and strengthens the whole brain. This means planning a classroom with many interesting activities requiring students to exercise the full range of creative and critical thinking skills—brainstorming, categorizing, hypothesizing, and so on.

Unfortunately, given the chock-full school day, there isn't a lot of time for providing a separate thinking skills program. And every savvy teacher understands that thinking activities practiced in isolation have little carry-over into the curriculum or real-world situations. TEN-MINUTE THINKING TIE-INS is designed to help you solve these problems.

In the following pages, you will find more than sixty quick, manageable activities that provide practice in over two dozen fundamental thinking skills ranging from analyzing to visualizing. These are the cognitive processes used by writers, scientists, artists, inventors, mathematicians, engineers, historians, teachers, and other smart people. (See the Resource section at the back of this book for a annotated list of the thinking skills.)

CONTENT AREA CONNECTIONS

Each activity relates to one or more content areas and can be integrated into your lesson plans. Along the way, students will develop such key skills as reading, writing, experimenting, observing, and drawing. As a bonus, the majority of the activities stress cooperative learning, which means that speaking and listening skills also get sharpened.

USING THIS BOOK

Learning to think is a nonlinear experience. Therefore, when choosing the activities that fit your needs, you may find yourself skipping from one part of the book to another.

The activities in this book are organized alphabetically rather than by thinking skill. This is because most of the activities simultaneously exercise several skills. For example, the activity "Fixing Directions" involves students in analyzing, sequencing, and troubleshooting.

If you want to put together a series of activities that zero in on one area of thinking, you can do that by consulting the index. There, you will find activities listed by type. For example, thirteen activities are listed under "Analyzing."

RESOURCES

Most of the activities require no outside materials. Many of them are accompanied by a page of starter ideas.

At the back of the book, you'll find several bonus resources including a list of read-aloud books useful for introducing specific concepts. There's also a set of suggestions for nurturing one of the most important of all the thinking skills: inventing.

BEYOND TEN MINUTES

If you want to invest more than ten minutes a day encouraging students to think, try the extension projects that accompany the activities. These follow-up activities can be adapted for whole-class work or for independent learning. They could even be sent home to involve parents in the development of their children's minds. (Now that's something to think about!)

ALIKE AND DIFFERENT

Careful thinkers spend much of their time **comparing** and **contrasting** pairs of things.

DIRECTIONS:
1. Pick a pair of things or processes that are related in two or more ways that students know about. Examples include city/country, fiction/nonfiction, or adding/subtracting. (See the next page for more pairs.)
2. Students, working alone or in small groups, think of ways the items are alike and different, listing as many as they can. (A simple grid can make the brainstorming easier.)
3. Have students pick—and then share—what they think is the most important similarity and dissimilarity.

EXTENSION:
Students give alike and different reports based on research. Possible items to compare and contrast are two cities, two kinds of vegetables, two famous leaders, two animals (lions/tigers), two heavenly bodies (moon/sun), or two similar historical events (assassination of Lincoln and assassination of Kennedy). Another option: alike and different autobiographies done by pairs of students.

Things to Compare and Contrast

adding/subtracting

adult/child

air/water

airplane/bird

airplane/boat

apple/banana

automobile/motorcycle

b (sound)/p (sound)

baseball (object)/football (object)

bath/shower

bike/skateboard

boat/car

book/magazine

book/teacher

boot/shoe

button/zipper

camera/eye

cat/dog

chair/sofa

circle/square

country/province or state

crying/laughter

door/mouth

door/window

drawing/photograph

ear/eye

egg/lemon

electrical cord/hose

fingers/toes

floor/ceiling

foot/hand

fork/spoon

globe/map

glove/sock

hammer/screwdriver

hand/foot

hat/roof

hearing/seeing

lake/river

letter/telephone call

lipstick/perfume

magazine/newspaper

moon/sun

pen/pencil

play/movie

radio/television

rain/snow

river/street

student/teacher

talking/writing

water/milk

yesterday/tomorrow

ALPHABET DESIGNS

Poets, puzzle makers, and advertising people all use **visual thinking** to surprise and delight their audiences. The activity, which provides practice **defining concepts**, may make students more aware of the use of creative lettering on posters, book covers, and other print media.

DIRECTIONS:
1. Demonstrate how lettering can reinforce the meaning of a word or phrase, for example:

   D
     O
       W
         N

2. Challenge students to creatively letter a variety of words with visual potential, such as *curve*, *slant*, or *steps*. (See the next page for more examples.)
3. Have students share the words on the board.

EXTENSION:
Teach students to create letter riddles known as *wordles*. In a wordle, word placement aims to convey a familiar phrase. Here's an example:

  don't step   or   don't step
  the line   ——————

This wordle represents the phrase "Don't step over the line." (Phrases that are relatively easy to translate into wordles appear on the next page.)

Words to Design

alone	short
big	slant
broken	slim
bumpy	separate
circle	smile
close	spread out
curve	stacked
eat	steps
fat	tall
fly away	thin
frown	touching
grow	up
little	zigzag
mountain	

Phrases to Turn into Wordles

bridge over troubled waters	reading between the lines
ham on rye	repeat after me
head over heels	somewhere over the rainbow
line up	standing under an umbrella
lull before the storm	stay behind the line
man overboard	time after time
one afternoon	upside-down cake
person under the weather	water over the dam
pheasant under glass	

ANIMAL-EYE VIEW

To you, it's just a mud puddle. But to a robin it's a source of life-sustaining water, while to a mosquito it's a maternity ward. To grasp these various realities, scientists and artists alike must practice the skill of **changing point of view**. The following activity also provides practice in **comparing** and **contrasting**.

DIRECTIONS:
1. While working on an animal unit, pick an object or an activity that one or more animals can relate to, for example: a garbage can, a picnic, or a rose. (See the next page for examples.)
2. Alone or in small groups, have students compare and contrast how humans and one or more animals see and feel about the thing. The comments could take the form of definitions. For example, a flea could define a dog as "a restaurant and hotel."

EXTENSION:
Compile a student dictionary written from the point of view of a single animal or an infant. For example, what might a dog have to say about such things as a leash, people, and TV? Another possibility is to present definitions of a single object from the point of view of many animals.

THERE'S NO PLACE LIKE HOME!

Things That Animals Might Encounter

automobile

clothing

dog (or other animals)

dog show

fishing hook

flowers

fly swatter

garbage dump

grass

honey

insect repellent

kite

lake

lawn sprinkler

leaf

light bulb

mirror

money

mud

picnic

rain

sewer

snow

spider web

telephone pole

tree

window screen

zoo

BY-HEART SPEECHES

Learning a passage by heart is an ancient but still powerful way to strengthen the skill of **remembering**. It also builds confidence while enriching every curriculum area.

Note: Ahead of time, have each student find and memorize a short poem, a story excerpt, or a passage dealing with a curriculum topic. The text could be student written or taken from a book, newspaper, or other publication. (See the next page for more sources.)

DIRECTION:
1. Divide the class into small groups.
2. Have students present their memorized passages. A reader in each group can follow the written passage in order to give the presenter prompting and feedback.

EXTENSION:
Have students deliver their memorized pieces as after-dinner presentations.

Items to Memorize

fables

folk tales

jokes

jump-rope jingles

lists such as
    African countries and capitals
    Asian countries and capitals
    bones in the human body
    Canadian provinces and capitals
    colors of the rainbow (in order)
    Dewey Decimal categories (10 major divisions)
    elements (hydrogen, oxygen, etc.)
    European countries and capitals
    Greek gods and goddesses (and their duties)
    mammalian orders (primates, carnivores, etc.)
    mountains (ten tallest)
    planets (from sun outward)
    rivers (longest)
    South American countries and capitals
    U.S. presidents in order
    U.S. states and capitals

play parts

poems

proverbs

song lyrics

speeches

stories

textbook passages

tongue twisters

trivia from books written for young people. Examples include Barbara Seuling's *The Last Cow on the White House Lawn & Other Little-Known Facts About the President* and Joseph Rosenbloom's *Bananas Don't Grow on Trees: A Guide to Popular Misconceptions.*

CALLING ALL SNOWFLAKES

No two snowflakes are exactly alike. Yet all snowflakes are similar in certain ways; for example, they all have six points or sides. **Generalizing** is the skill of finding features shared by a set of things. The activity involves **observing** and **comparing** and **contrasting**.

DIRECTIONS:
1. Divide the class into small groups and give each group several things or pictures of things that fit into a well-defined category drawn from a unit you are studying. For example, a category relating to transportation. (See the next page for other categories.)
2. Have each group list as many ways as they can that the things in the category are alike.
3. Students then write a statement that defines the category by explaining how all items in the category are alike: "All rivers have river banks, flow..."
4. Share the definitions orally.

EXTENSION:
Assign generalization reports based on research. An example would be a report about what all insects have in common, namely, a three-part body structure and a four-stage life cycle.

Things to Make Generalizations About

apples	maps
automobiles	months
baskets	myths
bicycles	newspapers
birds	noses
books	peanuts
buildings	pencils
buttons	people
candles	pianos
countries	playing cards
dictionaries	sandwiches
doors	schools
drums	seasons
even numbers	shirts
eyeglasses	shoes
fairy tales	stop signs
fingerprints	stories
flags (of countries)	tall tales
holidays	teddy bears
ice cubes	telephones
insects	tin can labels
jobs	triangles
light bulbs	vegetables
mammals	watches

CATEGORY MAKING

Classifying a collection of things into logical groups is an important activity used in science, business, law, and elsewhere. A good example is the system Melville Dewey dreamed up to catalog books in a library.

DIRECTIONS:
1. Pick a set of things to categorize, for example, animals. (See the next page for additional items.)
2. Have students, working alone or in small groups, think up as many ways as possible to group items within the set. For example, animals might be categorized:

   by use (companionship, food, research)
   by size
   by speed
   by habitat
   by longevity
   by friendliness

3. On the chalkboard, list all the categories the class comes up with.

EXTENSION:
Have small groups of students present reports on the same topic. Each report will deal with a different way of categorizing information.

Items to Categorize in Several Ways

automobiles
(where made, how used,
how expensive, etc.)

body parts
(use, size, mobility, etc.)

books
(use, size, popularity, etc.)

buildings

clothes
(use, material, cost, etc.)

community helpers

dreams
(content, scariness, length, etc.)

foods

friends

furniture

gifts

hobbies

inventions

jobs

movies

musical instruments

newspaper stories

pencils

pets

places

planets

plants

school subjects

smells

songs

sounds

sports

stories

tools

TV shows

vegetables

weather

words

CATEGORY SHAKING

Discoveries often come about by **classifying** objects in new ways. The discovery of penicillin is a famous example: while everyone else saw bread mold as just "mold," Alexander Fleming saw that it was a bacteria fighter. The activity provides practice in **observing** and **remembering**

DIRECTIONS:
1. Show students an ordinary object, for example, an orange. (See the next page for more items to re-categorize.)
2. Have students, working in small groups, create a list of categories in which the object could be classified. They should look for as many categories as possible. Silly categories are OK. For example, an orange can fit into the following categories:
- things to eat
- things that roll
- things that have their own packaging
- things that can go bad
- things that don't mind being squeezed
- things that grow on trees
- things that are orange
- things that sometimes have writing on them

3. Share the lists orally or on the board.

EXTENSION:
Have each student choose something to categorize and write a story, article, or poem called "The Many Lives of a _____."

Items That Fit Many Categories

advertisement

aunt/uncle

bear

blood

boat

bus driver

butterfly

canal

circus

computer

crayon

dentist

electricity

forest fire

gun

hat

hospital

insect

joke

king

leaf

mayor

money

mosquito

nightmare

pizza

poetry

rock

sandwich

siren

smile

soccer

spaghetti

spelling test

summer

supermarket

teacher

television

textbook

thunder

tornado

tree

water

whale

wind

word

zoo

DEBATABLE IDEAS

Because change is not always change for the better, inventors must move on to **evaluating** the worthiness of their ideas.

DIRECTIONS:
1. Write a debatable idea on the board. If possible, relate it to a topic of study, for example, "All African animals should immediately be placed in zoos to protect them from becoming extinct." (See the following page for additional topics.)
2. In small groups, have students discuss whether or not the proposition is a "good" idea. They should defend their opinions by giving examples of why the idea might or might not make sense.

EXTENSION:
Have students conduct full debates after researching the pros and cons of issues found in textbooks or the media.

Topics for Debate

Children should be allowed to run for president.

Children should be allowed to drive cars.

People should be able to be married at any age they like.

Picture telephones should replace regular telephones.

Students should be allowed to bring their pets to school.

Students should be able to choose their own teachers.

Students should wear uniforms to school.

TV viewing should be banned at night.

We should spend money putting a colony on Mars.

We should spend money building undersea cities.

No cities in the U.S. should be allowed to have more than 50,000 people.

There should be no speed limits on superhighways.

Instead of wars between armies, heads of countries should fight to settle differences.

Only adults should be allowed to have pets.

We should stop planting trees and invest in plastic factories.

People should be fined $100 for not voting.

No desserts should be allowed in school lunchrooms.

Police should be paid more than the city mayor.

No one should be allowed to own a gun.

Everyone should learn to use a computer.

No family should be allowed to have more than one car.

DEFINITION RIDDLES

Intelligent perception requires an awareness of details. The following activity develops that awareness as students practice **analyzing**, **classifying**, and **ordering**.

DIRECTIONS:
1. Share a few examples to teach the "definition riddle" format. In this kind of riddle, the riddler gives a series of clues, moving from general to specific. The first couple of clues should not give away the answer:

> Who is ...
> a man
> who was president
> during the war
> between the states?

> What is ...
> a kind of pet
> that barks
> and has a country in its name
> and rhymes with noodle?

2. Choose a riddle topic. (See the next page for examples.)
3. Have students work together creating riddles, which they can then share with the whole class.

EXTENSION:
Create definition riddle books that focus on particular subjects, for example, *Marvelous Math Riddles* or *Sensational Science Riddles*.

"IT'S A BALL"

"THAT YOU KICK"

"AND IT'S EGG SHAPED."

Subjects for Definition Riddles

airplane	mailbox
baseball	mirror
bathtub	moon (and other heavenly bodies)
bed	music
books	newspaper
cat (and other familiar animals)	nose
ceiling	playground
classmates	radio
clock	refrigerator
comb	robot
computer	sandwich (and other everyday foods)
convertible automobile	scientific tools
door	shirt
eyeglasses	sled
famous people	television
floor	traffic light
fork (and other eating implements)	vacuum cleaner
glue	water fountain
magnifying glass	window

DICTIONARY FOR E.T.

While pretending to explain words to an alien from outer space, students practice **defining concepts** and **changing point of view**.

DIRECTIONS
1. Brainstorm a list of items that might be a mystery to visitors from a distant planet. See the next page for examples or use words from a unit you are studying.
2. Choose one item from the list. Have students, alone or in small groups, write brief definitions explaining to the aliens what the thing is and how it is used. Students should imagine that the interplanetary visitors have no experience with the thing. For example, they don't know what a sandwich is, and they don't even know what eating is. Both the thing and the activity that goes with it must be explained.
3. Collect the explanations into a book.

EXTENSION:
Students can put on short plays in which aliens give "speeches" to their fellow aliens about objects that they found on earth.

Items to Explain to Extraterrestrials

bathtub

bicycle

bed

book

chair (or any other piece of furniture)

clock

computer game

crayon

dictionary

dollar bill

flag

fork (or any other eating implement)

hat (or any other type of clothing)

letters of the alphabet

measuring tape

numbers

perfume

piano (or any other musical instrument)

plastic dinosaur (or other toy)

radio

refrigerator

road map

roller skate

sand

sandwich

school

skateboard

swimming pool

telephone

television

tree

watercolor brush

worm (or any other animal)

DO-IT-YOURSELF QUIZ

When students create their own tests, they not only help the teacher, they also practice one of the basic thinking skills: **formulating questions**.

DIRECTIONS:
1. After presenting a lesson to the class, have students write their own individualized quizzes. These can involve short-answer questions, fill-ins, diagrams to label, open-ended questions, and so on.
2. Students should answer their own questions.
3. Have students exchange quizzes and then discuss the answers with their partners.

EXTENSION:
Invite students to submit questions for a quiz on a topic or book the entire class has been involved with.

DRAW AND TELL

Clear thinking often rests on skillful **observing**. Making a drawing or sketch is a proven observation technique.

DIRECTIONS:
1. Divide the class into pairs.
2. Give each pair two different objects, each related to a topic under study. For example, when teaching a unit about another culture, students might get two different artifacts. (See the next page for a list of other objects to draw.)
3. Have students make detailed drawings of their objects and then use the drawings to point out important parts of their objects. If students don't know the technical names of the parts, they can use descriptive terms. For example, the "eyelets" of a shoe might simply be called "holes."

Note: Students should not judge their drawings by prettiness. The goal is to create drawings that focus attention on details.

EXTENSION:
Students can write draw-and-describe reports that feature original student drawings of leaves, buildings, scientific instruments, or other things relating to the curriculum.

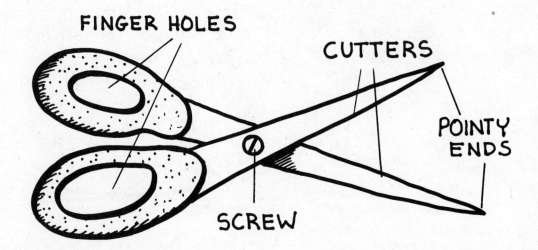

FINGER HOLES

CUTTERS

POINTY ENDS

SCREW

Subjects for Draw-and-Tell Reports

baseball

baseball glove

bicycle wheel

bone

city hall (or other building)

combination lock

computer keyboard

crystals

dollar bill

ear (outside)

earrings

eggbeater

eye

face of a cat or dog

fire hydrant

floor plan of the library

fruit—sliced in half

grater

gyroscope

hand

leaf of a tree

light bulb

map of the schoolyard, local park, etc.

microscope

model of airplane, boat, truck, etc.

musical instrument

painting

paper clip

scissors

sculpture

shoe

stapler

statue

telephone

VCR

whistle

EXPERIMENT PLANNING

Old science fiction movies make it seem that science requires fancy equipment. In reality, successful experimenting depends more on **formulating questions** and careful **observing** than on handling bubbly beakers.

DIRECTIONS:
1. Have students brainstorm questions that relate to familiar objects or happenings—questions that could be answered experimentally—for example, "Does music affect the rate at which plants grow?" or "Do different brands of cola really taste different?" (See the next page for other questions.)
2. Divide the class into small groups and have them think up an experiment that could answer the question. For example, an experiment about cola taste might involve blindfolding tasters and giving them samples in cups to avoid clues from distinctively-shaped bottles.
3. Have students share their experimental plans.

EXTENSION:
Invite students to carry out—and report on—experiments. Encourage the use of drawings to clarify their set-ups.

GRAVITY EXPERIMENT

Questions for Experiment Planners

Do some colors attract more attention than other colors?

Do plants need soil to grow?

Do plants need sunlight to grow?

Can a magnet attract something through water?

Can dogs understand words?

Is it better to study with or without music?

Do heavy objects fall faster than light objects?

Do different brands of detergent clean differently?

Do different brands of the same flavor of soda taste different?

Do "good citizenship" signs affect people's behavior?

Does drinking warm milk help people fall asleep faster?

Does the sense of smell have anything to do with the sense of taste?

Does eyesight have anything to do with balance?

Is it better to study for a test alone or with someone?

Does the temperature of the water affect how well soap works?

Does writing spelling words over and over lead to learning those words?

Can people send messages telepathically?

Can people judge durations (e.g., a minute) without looking at a watch? Are children or adults better at this?

Can people recognize faces by touch?

Does the direction that a top spins affect how long it spins?

Does the time of day affect how well students do on a test?

FIXING DIRECTIONS

Revising instructions is a **troubleshooting** activity that involves **analyzing** and **ordering**.

DIRECTIONS:
1. On the board, write a set of defective directions for doing simple tasks such as drawing a map, looking up a word in the dictionary, or taking part in a class discussion. Defects might include out-of-sequence steps, missing steps, irrelevant steps, or incorrect words. (See the next page for examples.)
2. Have students correct the directions and identify what was wrong with the original: wrong order, missing information, extra information, and so on.
3. Share the revised directions in small groups.

EXTENSION:
Have students create a flawed-directions bulletin board that challenges passers-by to spot the problems.

Flawed Directions

Finding a Book Needed for a Report
1. Go to the correct section of the library.
2. Pick a topic for the report.
3. Look up the book's number in the catalog.
4. If you see a friend, say hello.
5. If the book you are looking for isn't in, try to find another book that might do.

Brushing Teeth
1. Brush teeth.
2. Put toothpaste on brush.
3. Rinse mouth.
4. Put cap back on brush.

Solving a Textbook Word Problem
1. Look up the answer at the back of the book.
2. Do the arithmetic work required.
3. Make a diagram if that will help clarify the problem.
4. Read the problem to make sure you know what it's about.

Calling Someone on the Telephone
1. Dial or punch in the number.
2. Listen for the dial tone.
3. Say "Goodbye" when the other person answers.
4. Look up the number if you don't know it.

Batting in a Baseball Game
1. Watch as the ball approaches.
2. Get a good grip on the bat.
3. Swing.
4. Run to first base if you hit the ball.
5. Wave to your teammates if you make it safely to first.

Using a Pencil Sharpener
1. Turn the handle.

Making an Oral Report
1. Walk to the front of the room.
2. Look at the audience rather than at the floor.
3. Talk in a loud, clear voice.
4. Think about what you want to say.

FREEZE-DRIED FACTS

Getting information from a photograph, drawing, or chart involve**s observing**, **analyzing**, and **deductive reasoning.**

DIRECTIONS:
1. Present the students with a picture that carries a lot of information, for example, a photograph from *National Geographic* about a country you are studying, or a detailed illustration from a textbook your students are using.
2. Have students write as many facts as they can based on their observation of the picture.
3. In small groups, students share their fact lists and talk about any questions generated by the facts they found.

EXTENSION:
Give students frequent practice in reading information from maps, globes, and charts. For example, give students a detailed North American map and have them answer such questions as "Which is farther north, Chicago or Denver?", "When it's noon in Miami, what time is it in Dallas?", and "How many Canadian provinces are within 600 miles of Cleveland, Ohio?"

HALF A STORY IS BETTER THAN NONE

Deductive reasoning isn't a skill used only by detectives. At times most thinking people use their brains to fill in missing information. The following activity also provides practice in **predicting**.

Note: Ahead of time, have each student write a short paper about a familiar topic. It could be the plot of a popular movie or a summary of a topic studied in class. Each line in the paper should contain about six words. The total piece should be about ten lines.

DIRECTIONS:
1. Students should cut or carefully rip their paper from top to bottom, into two vertical strips. To make the activity easier, one strip should be two-thirds of the sheet.
2. Divide the class into pairs.
3. Partners exchange the wider strips of their papers and then try to figure out what the missing portions contain.
4. Have students compare their predictions with the originals. Point out that the goal is making sense rather than coming up with a word-for-word match.

EXTENSION:
Try the same activity using copies of paintings or photographs that are partly covered over. Students guess what the hidden portions show.

HOLE TRUTH

The ancient story of the "Six Blind Men and the Elephant" teaches a lesson that is still up to date: intelligent **observing** requires seeing the big picture as well as the details.

Before introducing this activity, read aloud and discuss "The Six Blind Men and the Elephant." You'll find the story on the next page.

DIRECTIONS:
1. On the board write the name of a thing that has two or more parts, for example, a chocolate donut, a flower, or a city. (For additional topics, turn to the page following "The Six Blind Men and the Elephant.")
2. List the parts of the thing or have the class brainstorm them with you. For example, a chocolate donut consists of pastry, chocolate frosting, and a hole.
3. Divide the class into groups. Each group should have at least as many students as the thing has parts.
4. In each group, assign one or more students to each part. Have them write a brief description of that part as if it were the entire object. For example, the student or students describing the donut hole might write:

> A donut is nothing at all, just air. You can't feel it. You can't see it. You can't taste it. You can't hear it.

5. Share the different paragraphs aloud or on a bulletin board. If there's time—or later on—have students create an accurate description of the whole thing.

EXTENSION:
Students, working alone or in groups, can create picture books in the pattern of "The Six Blind Men and the Elephant," replacing the elephant with other objects.

The Six Blind Men and the Elephant

Long ago in India, there was a group of six blind men who had been blind from birth. They wandered here and there, learning about the many interesting things in life.

One day, they felt the ground shake and they heard a bellowing noise. When they asked a villager about it, she said, "It's an elephant."

The blind men had never come across an elephant before. Because they wanted to know what this creature was like, they walked closer so that they could touch it.

The first blind man felt the elephant's long trunk. "Aha," he said, "this animal is a kind of snake. I can feel how it bends and twists."

The second blind man, who was standing next to one of the elephant's front legs, said, "You are wrong, my friend. I can clearly tell that an elephant is tall and round, like a tree trunk."

The third blind man laughed. He had found one of the elephant's tusks. "I don't know what you two are thinking about. It's plain that an elephant is a pointy beast shaped something like a spear."

The fourth blind man had climbed on the back of the third, and was examining the elephant's huge ear flap.

"Spear?" you say. "Where did you get that idea? An elephant is thin and floppy, like a blanket or a piece of parchment."

Meanwhile, the fifth blind man was touching the elephant's side. "I'm sorry to say that all of you are mistaken. An elephant is smooth and flat like a wall."

The last blind men had walked to the back of the elephant and had grasped its tail. "Listen," said he, "you know nothing of the truth. In fact, an elephant looks just like a piece of string."

By this time, lunch was served. The six blind men sat down, began to eat their food, and continued to argue about the true nature of the elephant.

Things with Parts

airplane

animal

apple

automobile

bike

book

bus

cassette player

chair

combination lock

compass

computer

desk

eye

felt-tip pen

fire engine

flower

galaxy

globe

light bulb

microscope

moon

pencil

pencil sharpener

piano

pulley

school building

scissors

seed

shirt

shoe

skates

skeleton

thermometer

tree

TV

vacuum cleaner

watch

HOW DOES IT WORK?

Describing the way something operates is a task that can involve a variety of skills including **remembering** and **analyzing.**

DIRECTIONS:
1. Choose an ordinary object, such as a pencil or a thermometer. It should be something whose operation students are familiar with. (See the next page for other examples.)
2. Have students, working alone or in small groups, briefly explain what the thing does and how it works.
3. Share the explanations.

EXTENSION:
Have students do research-based "how it works" reports answering questions that deal with curriculum-based processes, for example, "How does a lever work?" or "How does a telescope work?" In some cases, this research might include eyewitness observing.

Simple Things to Explain

How does a ...
> button fasten one thing to another?
> comb take out tangles?
> pencil write?
> safety pin fasten?
> strainer strain?
> tin can opener open a can?
> umbrella keep someone dry?

Complicated Things to Explain

How does a ...
> bat see in the dark?
> car's braking system stop a car?
> computer add numbers?
> crystal grow?
> digital clock keep time?
> duck swim?
> felt-tip pen write?
> firefly glow?
> fly manage to walk up a wall?
> freezer keep food from going bad?
> gasoline pump pump gas?
> jet plane fly?
> juggler juggle three (or more) balls?
> key unlock a lock?
> letter travel from one person to another?
> microwave oven cook?
> movie camera capture action?
> person sweat?
> piece of Velcro stick to another piece:
> planet stay in orbit?
> soap bubble take shape?
> spider spin a web:
> sponge take up and hold water?
> spring keep its shape?
> thermometer measure the temperature?
> traffic light know when to change?
> videotape camera record action?
> vacuum cleaner suck up dirt?
> whistle whistle?
> zipper zip?

HOW MANY WAYS?

Creativity often begins with the search for alternatives, one of which may prove valuable. In the following **brainstorming** activity, students try to think up alternatives to a familiar way of doing something.

DIRECTIONS:

1. Write a task or activity on the board. It could be a school routine—for example, taking attendance—or it could be a curriculum-related process, for example, creating laws. (See the next page for more examples.)
2. Ask students to brainstorm as many ways as they can for accomplishing the given activity. When finished, each student should identify a favorite way. This might be the quickest, most unusual, or most economical.
3. Share the ideas in small groups.

EXTENSION:

Have students report on inventions that changed how things were done, for example, the switch from gas lighting to electric lights.

NOSE
HOSE
CAR
WASH

Innovations Old and New

Tasks to Do in New Ways

answer the telephone
arrange a surprise party
avoid getting a sunburn
avoid boredom on a long trip
campaign for office
clean your bedroom
communicate with someone who doesn't speak your
    language
cut the grass
draw a picture
eat a sandwich
eat spaghetti
get rid of a telephone salesperson
get to school
give an oral report
greet a friend on the street
make up after an argument with a friend
organize clothes in a dresser
ride a skateboard
say "hello" or "goodbye"
see your reflection
shake hands
take a census
wrap a gift
wash a car
wash the dishes
wash the windows
watch TV
write a message (alternatives to using a pen or pencil)

Historical Innovations

campaigning (whistle stop versus TV)
communicating (Pony Express versus fax)
entertainment (vaudeville versus movies)
heating (fireplace versus central heating)
preserving food (salting versus canning or freezing)
travel (buggy versus automobiles)
waste management (garbage dump versus recycling
    center)

IMPOSSIBILITIES

Imagining the unimaginable is an **inventing** process that plays an important role in creative writing. For proof, we need look no further than to Lewis Carroll who claimed, "Sometimes I've believed as many as six impossible things before breakfast."

DIRECTIONS:
1. Present an ordinary object to the class, for example, an egg, a lock, or a felt-tip pen.
2. Ask students, working alone or in small groups, to brainstorm "impossible" qualities that the thing might have. Impossibilities relating to a felt-tip pen might include:
   - It will never run out of ink.
   - It can write stories all by itself.
   - It can draw pictures all by itself.
   - It dreams of turning into a computer.
   - It has memorized all of the writing in the world.
3. Have students share their ideas with the whole class.

EXTENSION:
Have students write short stories about impossibilities. Or, have them write reports about things that we now take for granted—airplanes, electric lights, videotape players—that once would have been impossibilities, known about only in the minds of dreamers.

INSIDE STORY

Scientists and poets often try to understand something by **imagining** that they are the thing. In the following activity, this approach to **changing point of view** provides practice in the literary skill of personification.

DIRECTIONS:
1. Choose a familiar thing, such as a chalkboard, or something from a unit of study, such as the heart. (See the next page for more examples.)
2. After thinking about—or observing—the thing for a few seconds, students write a series of statements that take the form of "I am" or "I know" or "I can."
3. Students share the statements in small groups.

EXTENSION:
Students can use their "inside" statements as starting points for research reports.

Objects to Personify

air

airplane

bicycle

bird

bus

camera

car

chair

clock

cloud

computer

dandelion

dictionary

dinosaur

door hinge

elbow

fire

glass

hair

hand

home

leaf

library

light bulb

lungs

map

moon

mud

musical instrument

nose

rain

school

sidewalk

skin

smoke

soap

stove

sun

teeth

telephone

television

thunder

tornado

volcano

water

wave

wind

INTERVIEW REPORTS

A Meet-the-Press-type presentation allows students the opportunity to take on the role of expert, while also sharpening the skill of **formulating questions.**

Note: Ahead of time, have each student prepare to be interviewed on a topic related to the curriculum—anything from Beijing to viruses.

DIRECTIONS:
1. The student "expert" announces the topic and gives a two- or three-sentence overview, for example: "Julius Caesar was the leader of the Roman Empire over 2000 years ago." There should be enough information in the overview to enable non-experts to think up questions about the topic.
2. Students, working in small groups, take a few minutes to frame questions on the topic. For example: "Was Julius Caesar the president of Rome?"
3. One at a time, groups ask their questions and the expert answers. (A scribe takes down questions that the expert can't answer without further research.)

EXTENSION:
If you have access to videotape equipment, tape these question-and-answer presentations. Play these "Meet the Press" programs at open house to help parents better understand your thinking-skills program.

INVENTING SUBSTITUTES

What do you do when it's raining but you don't have an umbrella? Or when a screw is loose but you can't find a screwdriver? Thinking people look for substitutes, a **problem-solving** task that involves **inventing**. The activity often comes into play in survival situations.

DIRECTIONS:
1. Choose something that most people use frequently, for example, a comb or Arabic numerals. (See the next page for a list of other things.)
2. Ask students to imagine that suddenly this thing is not available.
3. Have small groups of students brainstorm substitutes, for example, using fingers as a comb or tally marks to indicate numbers.
4. Share the ideas orally or post them on a bulletin board. Discuss the pros and cons of each substitute.

EXTENSION:
Publish a class-made book about substitutes with a title such as *What to Do When You Can't Find a* _____.
You might include stories based on research about historical substitutions, for example, the invention of nylon.

Replaceable Things

bag for carrying groceries

belt

cage for classroom pet

calculator

chair

clock or watch

desk for writing

dictionary

drawing compass

drinking glass

encyclopedia (particular volume needed for a report)

fork

gloves

hammer

hat

leash for dog

lunchbox

map

money

newspaper

paper and pencil

pencil sharpener

plug for bathtub

scale

screwdriver

shoe

shovel

shower

socks

television

thermometer

toothbrush

umbrella

vegetable strainer

wallet

window screen

IT'S "JEOPARDY!"

On the TV game show *"Jeopardy!"* contestants have to come up with questions that match answers. The game provides practice in both **remembering** and **formulating questioning**.

DIRECTIONS:
1. Read aloud a short nonfiction piece. Possible sources include your science or social studies text, a biography, or a current events magazine.
2. While you read, have students take notes, writing down interesting facts.
3. When you're done, have each student write at least one statement that refers to a fact but does not include the fact, for example:

   This is the smallest of the Great Lakes.

4. Have students present their statements in small groups, whose members take turn responding in question form: "What is Lake Ontario?"

EXTENSION:
Collect the "answers" for use later to play classroom *Jeopardy!* or to make a *Jeopardy!* bulletin board about a book or unit of study.

49

JUST THE FACTS, PLEASE

Clear thinking rests on knowing the difference between facts and opinions—the difference between **observing** and believing. The following activity is especially useful when introducing a topic or thing to be studied in depth.

DIRECTIONS:
1. Divide the class into small groups. Give each group an identical object, such as a metric ruler or a sheet of three-hole-punched notebook paper. (See the next page for more examples.)
2. Ask the students to write as many observations as they can about the object. Each observation should rely on one of the five senses and should be in the form of a sentence, for example:

> This sheet of paper has three holes.
> This sheet of paper has lines on both sides.

3. Students share their observations on the board. If a response seems not to be a fact, ask the student where the information came from.

EXTENSION:
Have students make fact reports, for example, "Ten Important Facts About Penicillin" or "Four Facts Everyone Should Know About Alligators."

Objects to Observe

In many cases, you'll need to use pictures of the objects.
Also, when working with measurable items, consider
providing students with rulers.

animal

automobile

ball-point pen

broom

building such as Taj Mahal

chair or stool

clock

coin

constellation, for example, The Big
  Dipper

crayon

dictionary entry

extension cord

geometric shape, for example, a
  trapezoid

hammer or other hand tool

hat or cap

light bulb

map

newspaper front page

painting or other work of art

paper cup

paper money

photograph of a distinctive place, for
  example, a stockyard

sieve

softball

title page from a book

videotape cassette

KEY WORD OUTLINE

Analyzing a piece of writing to get to the "heart of the matter" is a study skill valuable across the curriculum.

DIRECTIONS:
1. Give students a reading that has at least three paragraphs. Passages relating to a current topic of study should work well.
2. Have them write a key word or phrase for each paragraph and then add a sentence that explains the importance of the word or phrase in that context. For example, the key word in a paragraph about erosion might be *topsoil*. A student might write: "Topsoil can be washed away by water."
3. Share the outlines in small groups.

EXTENSION:
Have students write key-word outlines of their own reports or their classmates' reports.

LETTER TO THE EDITOR

Although **problem solving** is frequently thought of in terms of math and science, it also is a lifelong citizenship activity—especially when we communicate our proposed solutions in carefully thought-out letters.

DIRECTIONS:
1. Read aloud—or have students read—a newspaper article that describes a problem, for example, a dangerous intersection or damage to the ozone layer.
2. Have students, working alone or in small groups, brainstorm possible solutions they could write about in a letter to the editor.

EXTENSION:
On the board, write a group "letter to the editor" that sums up the students' solutions to the problem. Or have students, individually or in small groups, write the letters. For a variation, have students send problem-solving ideas to people in positions of authority, for example, the principal or the mayor.

LOOK BEFORE YOU LEAP

Because wishes sometimes come true, we need to think carefully about possible consequences. The following **predicting** and **deductive reasoning** activity relates to creative writing. That's because plotting stories often involves having characters struggle with problems they failed to anticipate.

DIRECTIONS:
1. Write a "what if" statement on the board, for example, "What if someone could be invisible?" (See the next page for additional iffy ideas.)
2. Have students, working alone or in small groups, brainstorm as many possible consequences as they can think of relating to the iffy idea.
3. Share the consequences.

EXTENSION:
Have students write "what if" stories. Another option is writing research reports; these might deal with the consequences of new laws, new medical discoveries, new inventions, and so on.

Iffy Ideas

What If You Could ...

answer any question

be any age

be friends with wild animals

be invisible

change something that happened

control dreaming

fly without equipment

grow big as a house or small as an ant

have a million dollars

have any wish come true

hear anything that anyone said

hit a home run every time at bat

know what was going to happen tomorrow

learn without studying

live on the moon

live without eating

meet anyone in history

never feel pain

never need sleep

read a million words an hour

read anyone's mind

see in the dark

speak every language on earth

star in a TV show

teach a dog or other pet to talk

travel anywhere in the universe

travel in time

turn into any animal

MEANING WHAT?

We can always look up a word's meaning, but writing fresh definitions gives practice in **analyzing** and **classifying**.

Note: Because creating definitions may be a completely new task for students, you may first wish to demonstrate the process a few times as a whole-class activity.

BLIZZARD
(NOUN) A WINDY STORM
THAT BLOWS SNOW SO
HARD, YOU CAN'T SEE
ANYTHING EVEN
DURING THE DAY.

DIRECTIONS:

1. Give the class a word to define. The word should relate to subject matter recently studied, for example, *volcano*.

2. Have students write original definitions. Many—but not all—words can be defined using the following format:

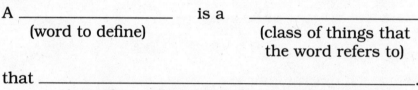

A _____ is a _____
   (word to define)   (class of things that
                              the word refers to)

that _____.
      (specific qualities that distinguish the thing
           from other members of its class)

For example:

> A volcano is a mountain-like land mass that is made out of lava which came up from deep underground.

3. Students share and, if they choose, revise their definitions. Point out that there is more than one right way to define any word. Variations depend on the features the writer chooses to emphasize. For example:

> A volcano is a mountain that has a crater at the top and that spews out hot rock and ash from time to time.

EXTENSION:
Students can make dictionary reports such as "Ten Key Words in *Tuck Everlasting*" or "A Dozen Octopus Words."

MISSING WORD DETECTIVE

When knowledge of a subject is incomplete, **analyzing** and **remembering** may enable thinkers to identify missing information. The process is as important in formulating scientific theories as it is in solving jigsaw and crossword puzzles. The following activity also can help improve reading comprehension.

DIRECTIONS:

1. On the board, write a statement relating to a topic of study, but insert blanks for a few words that can be guessed from the context. Use excerpts from textbooks, newspapers, or library books. Or make up your own texts as done in the following example:

> Write _____ statement on _____ board, leaving out _____ that can _____ guessed _____ the context.

2. Have students, working alone or in groups, try to fill in the missing words.

3. Share the results on the board. Ask students to state the clues that led them to discover the missing words. Be prepared to accept solutions that are logical even if they differ from the original. For example:

> Write *your* statement on *that* board ...

EXTENSION:

Have students make missing-word challenges for each other as a review of material studied in class.

MONDAY MORNING QUARTERBACK

Rewriting stories is an enjoyable way to practice **imagining.** It also gives practice in **problem solving.**

DIRECTIONS:
1. Read aloud—or have students read—a news report or short story. The story should include a decisive action. (Fairy tales, fables, or historical events work well.)
2. Students should think up two or three other ways things might have ended up if the person or persons had acted differently. (See "Story Ideas" on the following page.)
3. Have students choose one possibility and tell or write a new ending. This version might include the thinking of the main character or characters. (A sample story follows the "Story Ideas" page.)

EXTENSION:
Have students write alternative-ending book or movie reports.

58

Story Ideas

Cinderella: Cinderella doesn't lose the slipper.

Goldilocks and the Three Bears: The Bears decide to move away and never return to find Goldilocks.

Hansel and Gretel: The pair leave a trail of plastic checkers so that they can find their way home.

Rapunzel: The girl decides to cut her hair short.

Rumpelstiltskin: The girl tells her husband about the "funny little man."

Snow White: The magic mirror convinces the stepmother that she should not be jealous of Snow White.

Three Little Pigs: The wolf's doctor warns the wolf against huffing and puffing.

"I'll huff and I'll puff and I'll blow your house down," threatened the wolf.

"You'll never be able to," said the pigs.

The wolf tried but he found out that the pigs were correct. The house was still standing.

Then the wolf noticed the roof, and he thought, "I could climb up there and slide down the chimney. That way I'd be able to eat up the three pigs."

But then he had a different thought: "If I try to slide down the chimney, I might get stuck. I've read news stories about that kind of thing happening. And even if I don't get stuck, the pigs will hear me climbing up there and they might prepare a trap for me. Who knows? They could even put a kettle of hot water at the bottom of the chimney. I might get burned or worse. Forget that.

"So what can I do? I could tell them I don't want to eat them, and we could become friends. I'd like that because I don't have any friends. But I'm not sure that they would believe me, not right away.

"I know. I'll move to another town. I'll give up eating pig. I'll become a vegetarian. I like carrots and stuff like that. Then, when they hear that I've turned over a new leaf, they may come and want to be my friends. We could have all sorts of adventures together: The Big Better Wolf and His Three Pig Friends. Yes, it'll be wonderful."

The wolf then rapped on the door.

"We're not letting you in," said the oldest pig.

"I know that," said the wolf. "I just wanted to say goodbye. I'm moving away. But I hope to see you again. Best of luck. And tell your brothers I'm really sorry for destroying their houses. I'm going to get a job and I'll send them money for the repairs."

The wolf turned and walked away. The pigs scratched the hairs of their chinny-chin-chins and wondered if it was a trick.

"We'll see," said the oldest pig. "We'll see."

MOVE OVER, ANN LANDERS

Advice columnists demonstrate that **troubleshooting** and **problem solving** can be entertaining. Inviting your students to match wits with the experts can be a thought-provoking activity.

DIRECTIONS:
1. Find an advice column with a topic that's suitable for use in your class. Many real-world problems concerning the environment, ethics, jobs, and so on will have obvious links to your social studies or science curricula. For example, a column about talking in a movie theater raises a variety of issues about social behavior.
2. Read the problem part of the column aloud and have students write their proposed solutions.
3. After students share their writing in small groups, read aloud and discuss the columnist's advice.

EXTENSION:
Have students collaborate on an advice column for the school newspaper. (See the next page for ready-to-use problems.)

Problems for Advice Givers

School-related Problems

How to get ideas for writing a story

How to solve a particular kind of math problem

What to do when you are reading something and come upon a word you don't understand

How to study for a test

How to make friends after moving to a new school

What to do if you see someone cheating or misbehaving

How to work successfully on a group project

How to overcome nervousness when giving a speech

How to master tricky spelling words

Out-of-school Problems

How to think up gifts for family members and friends

How to break the TV-viewing habit

How to thank someone for a gift you don't really like

How to deal with a bully

How to make up with someone after an argument

How to say you're sorry when you've made a mistake

How to tell people that they're doing something wrong without making them angry

What to do if you're lost

How to say "no" to a telephone salesperson

What to do if you have a nightmare

How not to be envious of what other people have

How to break a bad habit

How to avoid being bored

MY NEWS

Sharing the news of our lives strengthens **remembering**. The following storytelling activity also provides practice in sequencing ideas, summarizing, using details, and other skills used in writing stories, poems, and plays.

DIRECTIONS:
1. Have students brainstorm several activities they did the day before.
2. Divide the class into two-person groups.
3. Have students give their partners one-minute accounts of one of their activities.
4. Have the partners then retell (or write) each other's stories. The original tellers can then check the accounts for accuracy.

EXTENSION:
Suggest that students provide dinner-time entertainment by retelling a story read aloud during class.

NEW USES FOR OLD THINGS

Nothing is totally new under the sun. Frequently, the secret of **inventing** is **brainstorming** new uses for old things.

DIRECTIONS:
1. Write the name of a familiar thing on the board, for example, "balloons."
2. Have students work in small groups to brainstorm new uses for that thing. For example, new uses of balloons might include spelling out words on a poster, packaging breakables, and hiding messages.
3. Share the "inventions" orally or on the board. (Later, you could make booklets concentrating on a single thing, for example, "Fifty Ways to Use a Toothbrush.")

EXTENSION:
Have students write reports about things that were used in ways very different from their original purposes, for example, light bulbs used to spell out words on a message board or fires used to send smoke signal messages.

PATENT PENDING

Looking for ways to improve the status quo is an **inventing** activity found in all fields. Innovative thinkers love to tinker with everything from gadgets to laws.

DIRECTIONS:
1. Choose an improvable thing or process from an area you've been studying. For example, if you're doing a unit on the human body, you might pick the eye (seeing). In a transportation unit, you might choose the airplane.
2. Have students, working alone or in small groups, think about and sketch possible improvements, for example, having the eyes on stalks so that a person could peer around corners.
3. Students share their concepts orally, describing their innovations and explaining why their innovations might be useful.

EXTENSION:
Have students suggest improvements on objects around the house, for example, the TV, the vacuum cleaner, or the sink.

Improvable Things

animal (barkless dog?)

automobile

baseball glove

bicycle

bread

CD player

character in a story

city

clothing

computer

crosswalk

elevator

fire alarm

game

garbage can

gasoline engine

gun

hairbrush

laws

mailbox

map

microscope

mirror

museum

musical instrument

newspaper

painting on a wall

plot of a story

school rules

stop sign

supermarket

swimming pool

textbook

thermometer

toilet

tree

zipper

PEAS IN A POD

Advancements in knowledge often result from **observing** the subtle differences between things that, on the surface, seem similar or even identical. The following activity also involves **comparing** and **contrasting**.

DIRECTIONS:
1. Give students pairs of similar objects, for example, two maps of the same region. (See the next page for more pairs.)
2. Have students list all the ways that the two things are really different. Their lists can include sketches. Note: In some cases, you might wish to provide students with tools that aid in making observations: magnifying glasses, rulers, scales, or thermometers.
3. Students share their observations in small groups or with the entire class.

EXTENSION:
Have students make research reports based on similar— but different—things, for example, the differences between a 747 and a DC10.

Almost-alike Things

apple halves (different varieties)

bricks

dogs of the same breed (e.g., two collies)

dollar bills

flowers of the same variety

fruit of the same type (two oranges)

human hairs (seen under a microscope)

keys to the same sort of lock

leaves from the same tree

linoleum tiles

map and aerial photo of the same place

paintings of the same subject

peas from the same pod

photos of similar Oriental rugs

pieces of wood from the same kind of tree

potatoes

thumbprints from two people

typefaces

PENNY FOR THEIR THOUGHTS

Thinking occurs in the brain, but it needn't remain hidden. The following **summarizing** activity gives students a view of the brain work done by classroom guests.

DIRECTIONS:

1. Arrange for a guest to give a short talk (five minutes or less) about the role that thinking plays in the person's work or hobby. The person might be a fellow teacher or a student from another class. You might invite someone from the community, such as a car mechanic or carpenter, but in this case you'd probably extend the length of the speech.

   As an alternative to a speech, you or a panel of students could interview the person in front of the class. (See the next page for a sample interview.)

2. In a "guest thinker" section of their notebooks, have students briefly summarize the presentation.

EXTENSION:

Create a "Local Thinkers Share Their Secrets" bulletin board. See Resources for examples of comments by a wide variety of thinkers.

Interview with a Thinker: A Plumber

Interviewer: Thanks for taking time to visit our class.

Plumber: I'm happy to do it.

Interviewer: We're interested in learning how thinking is used in different jobs.

Plumber: Thinking is definitely important in my work.

Interviewer: Can you give an example?

Plumber: Sure. Take when someone calls me up and tells me they have a problem. Often they'll be very upset. But I have to find out exactly what's wrong.

Interviewer: How do you do that?

Plumber: By asking questions. For example, the customer might say "The faucet is broken" but I don't know if that means that the water won't turn on or turn off. So I have to ask questions.

Interviewer: How else do you use thinking?

Plumber: Well, sometimes I won't have the exact part I need. For example, let's say I've got to replace an old washer in order to fix a leaky faucet. I carry lots of washers with me but sometimes I won't have the exact right one. Then, I'll compare and contrast those that I do have with the old one. This way I can usually find one that will work even if it's not perfect.

Interviewer: Can you give another example?

Plumber: You bet. Whenever I'm working on a tricky problem—like, say, a part that is stuck—I'll try to recall similar problems that I solved. If I can remember how I solved the problem the last time, that makes my work much easier. To me, remembering is definitely a thinking skill.

PERSONAL MAPS

Creating maps is a proven method for simplifying complexities. The task provides practice in visualizing and **translating**. While mapping is usually thought of as a social studies activity, it has important applications in science, for example, the mapping of other planets, the sea floor, and even chromosomes.

DIRECTIONS:
1. Ask students to brainstorm a list of significant places in their lives, for example, the classroom, the dentist's office, or a room in their homes.
2. Each student should choose one place and make a simple map (bird's-eye view).
3. Divide the class into pairs and have each map maker talk about the place.

EXTENSION:
Have students make maps of places that they encounter in stories, newspaper articles, and textbooks. These maps can be featured in map reports or chalk talks.

PICTOGRAPHS

Translating words into pictures is an ancient way of communicating ideas. **Defining concepts** visually is a language arts activity that also provides students with insights into the nature of our alphabet-based system of writing.

DIRECTIONS:
1. Write a sentence with between five and ten words on the board. It could be about the classroom, or it could be taken from the newspaper or a book.
2. Have students, working in small groups, translate the sentence into pictographs—diagrammatic pictures, each of which represents an essential word. Words such as "a" and "the" can be ignored.
3. Share the pictographic sentences on the board and discuss the similarities and differences.

EXTENSION:
Have students do research about the origins of the alphabet.

THERE'S A GOOD TV SHOW ON TONIGHT.

POSTCARDS FROM TINY WORLDS

The 1950s hit "Little Things Mean a Lot" could be the theme song for scientists, doctors, gardeners, airline mechanics, and others whose work often requires careful **observing** of little things.

DIRECTIONS:
1. Set up a microscope (or magnifying glass) "center." Once a week put a new slide under the microscope, for example, a bee's stinger, a piece of paper, or a leaf of lettuce. (See the next page for additional things to look at.)
2. Invite students to study and draw what they see.
3. At the end of the week, post the drawings.

EXTENSION:
Have students take their drawings home to share with their parents. At the end of the year, the drawings can be collected into "Books of Little Things."

DRAW WHAT YOU SEE

Little Things to Look At

bee stinger

blood cell

bread

chalk dust

cloth

cork

cotton ball

dandelion fluff

feather

fingernail

fish scales

fruit—inside, outside

grass

hair (animal, human)

leaf

mold on cheese

onion skin

paper

peppercorn

photograph from newspaper or magazine

rug fiber

salt

sand

seeds

soil

string

sugar

water

wood

yeast

QUALITY CONTROL

Taking stock of one's efforts plays a role in all fields.
Like other skills, **evaluating** improves with practice.

DIRECTIONS:
1. Pick an activity that all students have done, for example, making an oral presentation. (See the next page for more examples.)
2. Ask students, working alone or in small groups, to list specific actions that if done well would add up to a quality job. For example, a quality oral presentation might include giving valuable information, talking in a clear voice, and making eye contact with the audience.
3. Discuss or post the criteria.

EXTENSION:
Have students do research-based reports about the criteria for excellence in a variety of fields—teaching, police work, medicine, law, sports, manufacturing, service, and so on. Fresh information can be obtained by interviewing practitioners face-to-face or through the mail. As a culminating activity, publish a class book about standards for excellence in real-world jobs.

Activities to Evaluate

School Work

being in a play
conducting an experiment
doing library research
doing math homework
drawing a map
drawing a picture
giving a book report
making a diorama
making a graph
participating on a class trip
reading aloud
reading silently
running for a class office
taking notes from a book
taking part on a panel
working with a substitute teacher
writing a report

Out-of-school Work

baby-sitting
baking a cake
brushing teeth
carrying on a conversation
cleaning one's room
doing the dishes
doing the laundry
eating spaghetti
getting dressed (for school, for a special event)
giving a gift
making a model airplane
practicing a musical instrument
reading aloud
throwing a party
walking the dog
washing the car
washing windows
writing a thank-you note

RENAME GAME

Thinking up new names for something gives practice in **defining concepts** and **inventing**.

DIRECTIONS:
1. After studying a subject, ask students to come up with their own name for the thing, or names for the parts of the thing. For example, a geographical region known for raw materials might be called "Mineral Valley." The wing of a bird might be renamed "air pusher." (See the next page for more things to rename.)
2. Have students share their names orally or by combining them with pictures and then posting the results.

EXTENSION:
Create a class dictionary filled with renamed things. For example, the indentations on a golf ball might be called "unbumps."

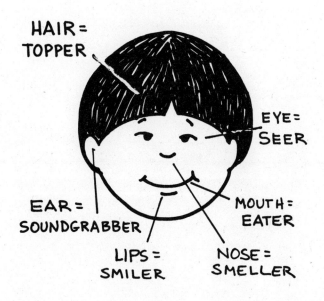

HAIR = TOPPER

EYE = SEER

EAR = SOUNDGRABBER

MOUTH = EATER

LIPS = SMILER

NOSE = SMELLER

Things to Rename

Note: Many of the items in this list have parts that could be renamed. For example, while the whole elephant could be renamed "earthwhale," its trunk might be called a "hose.")

animals (beaver = dam-maker)

body parts (hand = grasper)

book (Ugly Duckling = It's OK to Be Different)

building materials (bricks = stackers)

clock

clothing (hat = topper)

clouds

colors

foods

friends

furniture (chair = sitter)

games

geographical regions

geometric shapes (circle = roller)

historical periods

holidays

illnesses (flu = shivers)

jewelry

machines

movies (E.T. = I Want to Go Home)

pets

planets

rain

rivers

rocks and minerals

school

songs

sounds (thunder = skynoise)

sports

tools (telescope = skyglass)

TV shows

vegetables

SILENT TELEVISION

Here's an example of less being more. Showing a videotape without the sound stimulates **observing** and **deductive reasoning.**

DIRECTIONS:
1. Play a short videotape that includes narration or dialogue. You might use a one-minute excerpt from a science video or a TV commercial if you are studying advertising.
2. Have students describe what they see and guess what the words are.
3. Replay the tape so they can compare their guesses with reality.

EXTENSION:
Have students, working in groups, write original narration and dialogue (if any is needed) for a videotape. Play the tape while the students read their words.

SILLY SOLUTIONS

Every answer to a problem isn't necessarily good. That's why **problem solving** must involve the skill of **evaluating** solutions.

DIRECTIONS:
1. Present a silly solution to a serious problem the class has been studying. An example would be draining all the water out of a polluted lake to solve the pollution problem. (See the next page for other silly solutions.)
2. Working alone or in small groups, students should identify one or more reasons why the proposal is a bad idea. They should also include their own, possibly better, solutions.
3. Share the critiques and the alternative solutions.

EXTENSION:
Have students present panels or plays dealing with both the silly and the more sensible solutions.

Sample Silly Solutions

A student who can't solve a type of math problem tears the page with the problem out of the math book.

A reader who doesn't like the books written by a certain author asks the library to get rid of all of the books that the author has written.

A student arrives five minutes late for school. Rather than get a tardy note, the student goes back home.

Newspaper reports about how all the rain forests are being cut down upset many people. To make people feel better, the editor decides not to print any more such stories.

A student who always misspells a certain word decides never to use the word when writing a story or report.

A survey shows that many students find a certain subject hard to learn. Because the students are upset, the school board drops that subject from the curriculum.

Buildings around town are covered with graffiti. The city is getting so ugly that the city council requires owners to tear down the buildings.

Many library users forget to return their books on time. Therefore, the library committee makes a rule that books may be checked out for only an hour.

The smoke alarm keeps going off, so someone removes the whole alarm.

A painter has painted most of a room white but runs out of that color and decides to complete the job using yellow paint.

Someone who is bothered by a neighbor's barking dog tries to solve the problem by wearing ear plugs all the time.

Someone who is bothered by a squeaky door has the door removed.

Citizens are concerned about crime. To get money to hire more police, the citizens rob the local bank.

SOMETHING IN COMMON

Finding a common theme that links seemingly different things is a **classifying** skill that frequently involves **analyzing** and **finding patterns.**

DIRECTIONS:
1. Present students with a list of items that have the potential to be included in a group, for example: Paris, London, and Madrid. (See the next page for more examples.)
2. Students, working alone or with a partner, should name the group and propose one or more additional members. For example, the items in Step 1 may be categorized as "national capitals." Another item for that group would be "Rome."
3. Students share the results of the grouping. Make sure they understand that there may be more than one possible category. For example, the cities mentioned above could also be categorized as "European cities" or as "popular tourist destinations."

EXTENSION:
Have students create a "What's the Category?" quiz book or bulletin board.

Things to Classify

Reminder: There often will be more than one right answer.

blood, milk, soda (liquids)

drum, lightning, door, shoes (things that make sounds)

map, painting, dollar bill (things that include pictures)

Super Bowl, space shuttle blastoff, Jeopardy! (events that can be seen on TV)

fingernails, hair, grass (things that get cut)

surfboard, person, log (things that float)

baseball, basketball, soccer (team sports)

piano, banjo, violin (stringed instruments)

airplane, Rollerblade, railroad car (things that have wheels)

flying saucer, ghosts, time travel (things not everyone believes in)

donut, steering wheel, wedding ring (round things)

glue, nail, screw (things that fasten one thing to another)

fist, tin can, refrigerator (things that can hold other things)

flood, volcano, hurricane (things that can cause suffering)

laughter, crying, sighing (sounds that show emotions)

TV, vacuum cleaner, refrigerator (things that use electricity)

airplane, bird, smoke (things that move through the air)

dancing, singing, laughing (activities, -ing words)

sign, knee, Wednesday (words with silent letters)

mom, dad, noon (words that are spelled the same way backward and forward)

2, 4, 6, 10 (even numbers)

SOMETHING'S MISSING

Imagining alternative realities enables us to develop coping strategies. It also exercises the skills of **predicting** and **hypothesizing**.

DIRECTIONS:
1. Pick an essential activity, service, law, organization, or institution that plays a role in the lives of students, for example, "going to school" or "electricity."
2. In small groups, have students discuss what life would be like if that "thing" no longer existed. You might ask questions such as "How would you get along?" or "What other things would be changed?"

EXTENSION:
Have students write reports on how things used to be before the arrival of a specific invention such as the TV, the telephone, indoor plumbing, and the computer.

What If There Were No ...

churches or temples

electricity

food stores

garbage collection services

hospitals

insurance

laws

    child-protection laws

    littering laws

    noise laws

    traffic laws

libraries

movies

museums

natural gas pipelines

newspapers

parks

police

ready-to-wear clothing

recordings (CDs, audiotapes)

running water

schools

scouting organizations (Boy Scouts, Girl Scouts, etc.)

telephones

television

weather reports

SPELLING PATTERNS

Finding patterns and **generalizing** from these patterns is a major thinking skill that can be applied to many curriculum areas.

DIRECTIONS:
1. On the board write a group of words that share the same spelling pattern. For example:

    cry...cries
    fly...flies
    spy...spies

(See the next page for more examples.)
2. Ask students to state the pattern as clearly as they can. For example, "When a word ends in *y* and that *y* has a consonant before it, change the *y* to *ie* before adding *s.*"

    If possible, students should add additional examples to the original collection, for example, *try.*

EXTENSION:
Compile a class book of spelling tips based on the patterns students identify.

Spelling Patterns to Describe

believe, friend, lie, retrieve

conceive, deceive, receive

hop/hopping, nap/napping, cut/cutting, beg/begging

hope/hoping, name/naming, bite/biting

box/boxes, fox/foxes, tax/taxes

illegal, illegible, illogical

mislead, misspell, mistake, misunderstand

uncertain, unkind, unnecessary, unusual

knife/knives, life/lives, wife/wives

Jan's bike, the dog's dish, the friend's book

immature, immediate, immobilize

can't, don't, won't, shouldn't

English, French, German, Spanish (all begin with capital letters)

STARTING POINT

An early step in studying any topic is assessing what we already know. **Remembering** leads to greater involvement in the learning process, especially when paired with **formulating questions** about what we would like to learn.

DIRECTIONS:
1. Present a topic that students will be studying, for example, the moon.
2. Have students brainstorm facts that they already know about the topic. At the same time, they should list questions that they'd like to have answered.
3. Pool the facts orally and record them on chart paper.

EXTENSION:
Encourage students to conduct independent research on a topic. (See the next page for possibilities.) Have them begin this project by using the same strategy—listing known facts and questions.

Starting Point Topics

Africa

animal

astronomy

automobile manufacturing

ballet

Bill of Rights

calendar

desert (Gobi, Sahara, Painted, etc.)

dictionary

egg

fire

flu

food (pizza, peanut butter, etc.)

earthquakes

farming

food groups

gold

hometown

job (engineering, military service nursing, etc.)

laws

lightning

Lincoln

magnet

making movies

Mars

money

musical instrument

newspaper (what it contains, how it's organized)

oceans

piano

police

principal of a school (what the job consists of)

punctuation

rainbow

river (Nile, Rhone, etc.)

skin

soap

soil

teenage years

tepee

tongue

vegetable

war

water conservation

wind

winter

TAKE A CLOSER LOOK

Zooming in on a subject can be a effective **observing** strategy.

DIRECTIONS:
1. Give each student an easy-to-draw object, preferably one that relates to a curriculum subject. Examples include the hand, a leaf, a feather, or a photocopy of a dollar bill.
2. Students draw the object in a way that fills an entire page, then choose a part of that drawing and make another full-page drawing that shows the part. They continue until time is up and then share their drawings in a small group.

EXTENSION:
Make a book of zoom-in drawings. Depending on the item, students might use magnifying glasses or microscopes.

TELL IT LIKE IT IS

A simile explains one thing by **comparing** it to something familiar: "A period is like a stop sign because it stops readers at the end of a sentence." This activity helps students grasp concepts in all curriculum areas.

DIRECTIONS:
1. Write a simile on the board, for example: "A mirror is like a friend because..." (See the next page for more simile starters.)
2. Have students, working alone or in groups, finish the simile by explaining the connection, for example: "A mirror is like a friend because a mirror gives you information you need to look your best."
3. Share the completed similes. Note: There may be more than one way to complete or explain a simile.

EXTENSION:
Have students create their own similes to explain personal topics ("My vacation was like _____ because...") or curricular topics ("The kidneys are like _____ because...").

A LIBRARY IS LIKE A GARDEN BECAUSE...

Simile Starters

The circulatory system is like a railroad because ...

A white blood cell is like a soldier because ...

School is like a factory because ...

School is like a department store because ...

The mouth is like a door because ...

A person's skin is like a bag because ...

TV is like a drug because ...

TV is like a parent because ...

A dream is like a movie because ...

A short story is like a baseball game because ...

A sentence is like a brick because ...

The library is like a garden because ...

A smile is like a key because ...

Anger is like a fire because ...

A book is like a friend because ...

Clothing is like a house because ...

A writer is like a painter because ...

Mathematics is like a language because ...

A spider is like a person who is fishing because ...

A bank is like a refrigerator because ...

A law is like a river's banks because ...

A book is like a storage cabinet because ...

A computer is like a worker because ...

TEXTBOOK TINKERING

Translating a message from one language or form to another is a powerful brain boosting activity. It also is a vital study skill.

DIRECTIONS:
1. On the board, write a sentence or two from a textbook you are using.
2. Underline the key words and phrases.
3. Have students rewrite the passage in their own words. While they can use unimportant words such as *the* from the original, they should try to paraphrase the underlined expressions.
4. Have students share their paraphrases with partners.

EXTENSION:
Have students create nonfiction picture books for younger children. These books can be adapted from textbooks or magazine articles. Point out that it's OK to use some big words while simplifying material, but that these difficult words should be explained.

THIS IS TO THAT

Relating one pair of things to another pair is a challenging form of **comparing**. The skill is especially important in dealing with math and science topics.

DIRECTIONS:
1. Write an analogy on the board, for example: wing is to bird as fin is to fish. With older students, you might use the notation found in national tests:

   wing : bird :: fin : fish.

In this case, read the analogy aloud to show what the symbols mean. (See the next page for more examples.)
2. Have students write a brief statement explaining why the analogy is true, for example:

   The wing is used by the bird to move from one place to another. In the same way, the fin is used by the fish to go where it wants to go.

Note: There usually are many right ways to explain or interpret an analogy.
3. After students share their explanations in small groups, lead a class-wide discussion to make sure that everyone understands the relationship.

EXTENSION:
Give students partial analogies to complete and then explain. Leave out one or two elements:

   Buick : *car* :: *Quaker Oats* : _____?_____

Sample Analogies

egg shell : yolk :: orange peel : orange pulp

A : B :: one : two

point : pencil :: blade : knife

hose : firefighter :: brush : painter

toothache : tooth :: fire alarm : school

red : colors :: Monday : days of the week

wheel : car :: foot : person

finger : hand :: toe : foot

food : person :: gasoline : automobile

cold : refrigerator :: warm : furnace

eye : seeing :: ear : hearing

chair : sitting :: bed : sleeping

talking : hearing :: writing : reading

map : city :: portrait : person

beginning : ending :: top : bottom

stamp : letter :: coin : pay telephone

teacher : student :: doctor : patient

THIS IS WHERE I CAME IN

We often find ourselves coming into things in the middle. That experience stimulates **analyzing** and **predicting**.

DIRECTIONS:
1. Read a short passage from a story or article, but start in the middle. Nonfiction picture books work well.
2. When you reach the end, break the class into small groups and have students talk about what they thought the first part of the piece covered. Their ideas may not be the same as those in the original work.
3. Now read the piece from the beginning.

EXTENSION:
Try the same activity when playing videotapes.

THREE DAYS LATER, THE TALKING SNAIL...

TOMORROW'S NEWS TODAY

Gazing in a crystal ball isn't the only way to get a sense of the future. The following current events activity relates **analyzing** available information to **predicting** upcoming happenings.

DIRECTIONS:
1. Read aloud a newspaper article about a current event that is likely to be in the news for a while, for example, a major flood, transportation accident, or space mission.
2. With the class, brainstorm several possible results of the event. List the possibilities on the board.
3. If there's time, students can write short "news briefs" for the next day's paper. Post these predictions so students can compare their ideas.
4. The next day, read and discuss the follow-up article.

EXTENSION:
Have students write "prediction reports" based on research. Examples include "Cars of the Future" or "Tomorrow's Telephones."

TOUCH AND TELL

The thinking person uses all senses for **observing**. The following sensory-description activity develops skills that are important for the young scientist and writer.

DIRECTIONS:
1. Choose an object that consists of several parts and/or textures, for example, a candle. You might choose an item specifically to introduce a unit of study, for example, a lightbulb with a unit on electricity, or an acorn with a unit on trees.
2. Divide the class into two-person teams and give each team one object hidden in a paper bag.
3. One person on the team will reach into the bag, touch the object, and describe it in detail while the other person transcribes the description. Make sure students know to go beyond identifying the object. The idea is to report as many details as possible: "It's got a tube-like part that's slippery; this part is as thick as my thumb. The thing also has a stringy thing at one end."

EXTENSION:
Students write picture books that invite readers to use different senses to observe things. Another option is writing short stories in which characters have to use the sense of touch or other senses to get out of predicaments.

TWENTY QUESTIONS

In the days before TV turned parlor games into spectator sports, activities like "Twenty Questions" gave people a chance to sharpen their **remembering**, **analyzing**, and **classifying** skills.

Note: You may wish to model the activity for students who aren't familiar with it. See the example on the following page.

DIRECTIONS:
1. Pick a thing that the class has studied, or have a student "quiz master" to do the picking.
2. The presenter classifies the thing as animal, vegetable, mineral, or a combination.
3. Have a team of questioners—it could be the entire class—try to guess the subject by asking up to twenty questions that can be answered by "yes" or "no."
4. To settle disputes, form a "panel of experts" who will decide whether a question should get a "yes" or "no."
Hint: If a question can't be answered with a "yes" or "no," ask the questioner to rephrase it. If the host doesn't know the answer, he or she should admit it.

EXTENSION:
Remind parents about this excellent after-dinner game by playing it at a back-to-school night.

IS IT BIGGER THAN A BREADBOX?

Twenty Question Demonstration

Subject: bicycle chain

Host:	I'm thinking of something that is mineral.
Question 1:	Is it manufactured?
Host:	Yes.
Question 2:	Is this part of something else?
Host:	Yes.
Question 3:	Is this one single thing?
Host:	Yes.
Question 4:	Is this thing used in the house?
Host:	No.
Question 5:	Is it used in business?
Host:	Yes. Sometimes.
Question 6:	Then it can also be used for fun?
Host:	Yes.
Question 7:	Does this thing move?
Host:	Yes.
Question 8:	Does it make a noise?
Host:	Rephrase the question, please.
Question 8:	Is its purpose to make a noise?
Host:	No. What were you thinking of?
Question 9:	A bell. But anyway, is this thing made up of parts?
Host:	Yes.
Question 10:	Do lots of people own this thing?
Host:	Yes.
Question 11:	Do lots of people in this room own one?
Host:	Yes.
Question 12:	Do kids bring this thing to school?
Host:	Yes.
Question 13:	Do they bring it into the school room?
Host:	No.
Question 14:	Do they leave it outside?
Host:	Yes.
Question 15:	Is this thing part of a bicycle?
Host:	Yes.
Question 16:	Is it a bicycle chain?
Host:	That's it.

TWO PLUS TWO ISN'T FIVE

All mathematicians make mistakes. The thinking mathematicians are simply better at **troubleshooting** their work. This involves locating errors and figuring out how they were made. The process can be easily practiced on a daily basis.

DIRECTIONS:
1. Write an incorrectly worked-out math problem on the board. It could be something as simple as an addition or multiplication problem. Or it could be a word problem. The error could be computational, for example, forgetting to carry. Or it could be conceptual, for example, misunderstanding what the problem is asking for.
2. Alone or in small groups, have students study the problem, locate the error, and write a correction.
3. Lead a whole-class discussion to make sure everyone understands what went wrong and how it should be fixed.

EXTENSION:
Have students create problems for classmates to troubleshoot. These could be featured on an ongoing bulletin board or collected in a *Find and Fix* book.

TWO-TRACK MIND

Learning to look at issues from two or more sides gives practice in **changing point of view** as well as **evaluating**.

DIRECTIONS:
1. Write an opinion on the board, for example: "Reading a story is better than watching a movie of the same story." (See the next page for additional topics.)
2. Working alone or with partners, students list as many reasons as they can that support and contradict the statement.
3. Students share their lists with the entire class.

EXTENSION:
Have each student state an opinion—for example, "June is the best month"—and then write an essay defending an opposing opinion.

Two-sided Topics

Animals: Animals should have the same rights as people.

Cleaning up: Taking a bath is better than taking a shower.

Food: Bananas are the best fruit.

Geography: Rivers are more interesting to study than oceans.

Height: It's better to be tall than short.

Money: Paper money is more useful than change.

Music: The piano makes prettier music than the trumpet.

Pets: Dogs make better pets than cats.

Pictures: Photographs are more interesting to look at than paintings.

Schools: Students should attend school through the entire year.

Season: Winter is the best season.

Security: A combination lock is better than a key lock.

Sky: The sun is more exciting to study than the moon.

Smell: Flowers smell better than food.

Space exploration: We should spend money exploring outer space.

Sports: Baseball is more fun to play than football.

Television: TV viewing should be limited.

Transportation: Biking is safer than skateboarding.

Voting: Elementary students should be able to vote in national elections.

Weather: A snowstorm is scarier than a thunderstorm.

Writing: A pen is a better writing tool than a pencil.

WHAT REALLY HAPPENED?

Smart people understand that **remembering** isn't one hundred percent accurate. Recognizing the pitfalls of memory provides motivation for checking and rechecking the facts.

A few days ahead of time, read aloud a short story. You could use a newspaper report or a dramatic passage from a textbook, for example, the story of a scientific discovery.

DIRECTIONS:
1. Divide the class into pairs. Ask students to tell each other as much of the story as they can remember.
2. Reread the original story so that students can evaluate their memories.
3. Have students individually write about the differences between their versions and the actual story or report.

EXTENSION:
Give this activity a visual twist by having students try to remember as much as they can of a detail-rich painting, photograph, or diagram.

WHAT'S INSIDE?

Some of the greatest scientific minds of the twentieth century used indirect methods to identify the mysterious parts of the atom's nucleus. The following **deductive reasoning** activity is a low-tech version of their efforts.

DIRECTIONS:
1. Inside a well-sealed cereal or shoe box place several things that will make a noise when shaken. The items can be all of the same kind, for example, half a dozen marbles. Or you can mix several different things, for example, a marble, three checkers, and a chain.
2. Invite students, in small groups, to shake the box and try to identify what's inside. Students should include their reasons, for example, "I heard rolling sounds, which could be made by marbles."
3. After everyone in the room has had a chance to work with the box, share the contents with the students. Note: Wrong guesses may show as much intelligence as correct guesses.

EXTENSION:
Invite a doctor to visit the class and talk about techniques for examining the body from the outside.

Things for a Mystery Box

apples

bells

books

bottles

bottle caps

checkers

children's blocks

coins

combs

crayons

dice

forks

golf balls or Ping-Pong balls

keys

marbles

nails

paper clips

pencils

playing cards

plastic cups

screwdriver

screws

shoes (baby)

stones

thread spools

tin cans (small ones)

WHAT'S MY RULE?

Winter follows autumn which follows summer which follows spring. Seed leads to sapling leads to tree leads to seed. **Finding patterns** like these is often a step in **defining concepts**. It's also a vital skill in making sense of the world we live in.

DIRECTIONS:
1. Present the class with an item or a series of items that fit into a pattern, for example, a checkerboard. (See the next page for more examples.)
2. Have students, working alone or in groups, describe the pattern. In some cases, using imperative sentences works best. For example, here's a rule for describing the checkerboard pattern:

> Follow a red square with a black square and a black square with a red square. Put eight squares in a row. Make eight rows. Let red squares touch other red squares only at corners.

3. Have students share the pattern descriptions on the board or orally. It's likely that there will be more than one valid way to describe a pattern.

EXTENSION:
Make a bulletin board featuring patterns found around the school, the neighborhood, and the town.

Patterns to Consider

astronomical events
   tides
   waxing and waning of the moon

bead sequences
   color
   shape
   size

codes
   letter substitutions: a = b, b = c, c = ?
   number substitutions: a = 1, b = 2, c = ?

fabric patterns

glassware decorations

literary patterns found in repetitive books like
   Green Eggs and Ham by Dr. Seuss
   The Grouchy Ladybug by Eric Carle
   If You Give a Mouse a Cookie by Laura Numeroff
   Millions of Cats by Wanda Gag
   Poor Esme by Victoria Chess
   Tikki Tikki Tembo by Arlene Mosel

numerical sequences
   1, 2, 4, 8, 16, 32
   1, 3, 2, 4, 3, 5, 4, 6

spelling patterns (see "Spelling Patterns" activity)

temporal sequences
   day, night
   Monday, Tuesday ...
   January, February ...

wallpaper art

weather patterns
   rainfall during the year
   temperature during the day and the year

WHY DO MOSQUITOES BUZZ?

Hypothesizing is just a fancy word for intelligent guessing based on previously acquired knowledge.

DIRECTIONS:
1. Pose a question about a subject that students have some familiarity with, for example, "Why do books have page numbers?" (See the next page for more questions.)
2. Students try to reason out an answer. An advantage of working in groups is that students can pool their knowledge.
3. Share the hypotheses and discuss ways that the answer might be learned through research or experimentation. Note: Some "wrong" hypotheses will exhibit intelligence and creativity.

EXTENSION:
Do the same activity as a way of introducing a new unit. For example, you might begin the study of trees by asking "Why do leaves change their color in the fall?" After students have given their reasoned guesses, they should evaluate their hypotheses through research. Their findings can be presented orally or on posters or as booklets.

Why do ...

babies cry?

bicycle wheels have spokes?

books have page numbers?

bricklayers lay bricks off center?

cans of food usually have a round shape?

cars have license plates?

cats have whiskers?

ceiling tiles with holes have holes?

coins have dates printed on them?

crayons have paper coverings?

dollar bills have serial numbers?

donuts have holes?

electric plugs have two (or three) prongs?

fingers have fingerprints?

flowers have colors?

houses have windows?

letters come in both uppercase and lowercase?

people have two ears?

pianos have black and white keys?

rattlesnakes have rattles?

schools have fire drills?

    ... principals?

    ... report cards?

    ... summer vacations?

shoes with tongues have tongues?

suit jackets have buttons on the sleeves?

stop signs have eight sides?

tables usually have four legs?

teeth come in different shapes?

telephones have letters on some of the buttons?

words with silent letters have silent letters? (e.g.,

    Why is there a "d" in Wednesday?)

Note: For more "good questions," see *Why Do Clocks Run Clockwise and Other Imponderables* by David Feldman.

THE WINNER IS ...

Experts love to publish "ten best" lists of things like cars, movies, restaurants, and cities. The goal of this activity is not to discover the actual "best" but rather to exercise the skills of **evaluating** and **ordering**.

DIRECTIONS:
1. Choose any category that has the potential for a "ten best" list, for example, "The Ten Most Interesting Countries." (See the next page for more examples.)
2. Students should think up one or more criteria to be used in picking the best of the bunch.
3. Have students, working alone or in small groups, make their selections. (They don't have to come up with ten entries. A list of three items is long enough to give evaluation practice.)
4. Discuss the findings with the whole class.

EXTENSION:
Create a "ten best" bulletin board or a "ten best" column for the home-school flyer. Another option, near the end of the school year, is to publish a series of lists: favorite lessons, favorite library books, things to change next year, and so on. These student-made lists could give you valuable planning information.

Categories

Note: Working with many of the following categories will require research.

actors

animals with natural camouflage

authors

books

Canadian prime ministers

characters in books

clothing stores

colors

comic strips

computer games

days of the week

desserts

fast-food restaurants

field trips

flowers

games

hobbies

jobs

months of the year

scary movies

singers

sports

TV shows

U.S. presidents

vegetables

weekend activities

WONDER-FUL THINGS

At age five, Albert Einstein was given a compass by his father. Years later, Einstein said that **observing** that device and **hypothesizing** about its miraculous behavior led him to devote his life to probing the mysteries of nature. There's no guarantee that filling your classroom with intriguing things will create Nobel Prize winners. But maybe ...

DIRECTIONS:

1. Once a month—or oftener—bring a "miraculous" object like a compass to your classroom. Most of the objects listed on the following page are inexpensive. Costlier items can often be borrowed from science museums or practitioners. For example, a doctor might loan the class an old stethoscope.

2. Make the object available for students to examine, play with, and use. You can heighten their interest by posing simple questions such as:

   What do you see?

   How do you think the thing works?

   What would you like to know about the thing?

3. Have students contribute to a chart about the object. The chart can have a "What I Know" section and a "What I'd Like to Know" section.

EXTENSION:

Encourage students to answer questions from the chart and orally report their findings to the class.

Wonder-ful Things for Children to Encounter

ant farm

balance scale

barometer

beehive

binoculars

compass

electrical circuit with bell

flashlight

flipbook (animation drawings)

gyroscope

kaleidoscope

light meter

Magic Slate (toy)

magnet

magnifying glass

money from another country

motion picture film

music box

pattern blocks

pendulum

photo-sensitive blueprint paper

prism

Slinky

soap bubbles

spinning top

stethoscope

sundial

thermometer

tuning fork

wind chime

wind sock

ONGOING PRACTICES

The following ideas are meant to support and enhance routines that may already be in place in your classroom.

Flow Charting: Any extended school activity—for example, carrying out a science project or putting on a play—gives students a chance to master the art of flow charting. This important planning procedure involves analyzing an upcoming activity and describing or picturing each key step in a separate box. Whenever there is the possibility of a choice ("If pumpkin seeds aren't available, I'll use lima beans), arrows are used to indicate alternative paths.

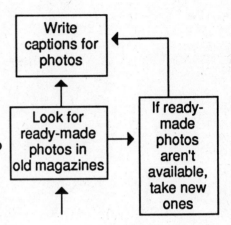

Flow charting can also be used as a troubleshooting tool to review a process that isn't working and to think up options to test.

Graphing: Many in-school and out-of-school happenings provide opportunities for collecting, organizing, and picturing data for the purpose of analysis. Examples of data to graph include:

- student attendance data
- numbers of books circulated by the library
- weather facts (precipitation, temperature)
- business facts (rise and fall of stocks)
- news events as reported in the newspaper (fires, car crashes, etc.)

If students are too young to create their own individual graphs, helping the teacher create a class model can serve as a good introduction to this important process.

"I Wonder" Bulletin Board: You can nurture the important habit of asking questions by maintaining a bulletin board on which students—and adults—can share whatever puzzles them. Use these questions to spark classroom discussions or as starting points for reports. (If your students are too young to make reports, pass their questions on to older students who can then appear as guest lecturers in your room.)

Learning Reviews: One of the easiest—and yet most powerful—ways to motivate thinking is to end your lessons (or periods of study in a textbook) by giving students a few minutes to write about what they learned. This writing can be free, or you can structure it

by suggesting prompts such as:
- What's the most important fact you learned?
- Write your own definition of _____
- Make a diagram of _____ and label the parts.
- What questions do you have about _____?

Students might share their results in small groups.

Letter Writing: Encourage students to write letters to business people, politicians, inventors, and other people in the news, asking them to explain the thinking behind their actions. For example, a student might write to a coach asking about the rationale for making a particular decision in a game or for trading a player.

Self-evaluation: Like charity, evaluating should begin at home. Whenever students create an original piece of work—a poem, a map, a science project—they should complete it with their own assessment of the work.

When you give an assignment, be sure to present a list of the criteria for excellence. For example, criteria for a graph project might include giving the graph a descriptive title, using different colors for each category, and writing a one-paragraph summary.

Have students discuss their work in relationship to the criteria. They should then submit their evaluations with the finished project.

"Thinking" Reports: Have students give reports on inventions, discoveries, and other creative works that involve thinking. Stories behind such things as the safety pin, the laser, frozen food, and the Sistine Chapel can serve as memorable examples of how the mind really works. Such real-world accounts also illustrate the value of persistence, cooperative effort, and other productive strategies.

Webbing: An effective brainstorming technique is to capture ideas graphically. This strategy, also known as "clustering," gets ideas flowing while simultaneously suggesting relationships. It thus sets the stage for organizing material.

Webbing is commonly used in the pre-writing stage of preparing reports, essays, and other nonfiction forms.

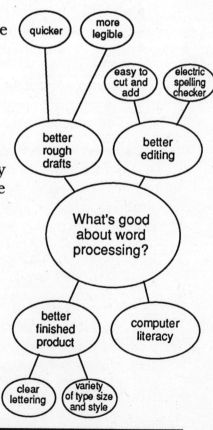

Thinking Skills Defined

The brain works holistically. When given any task—for example, recognizing a face, or figuring out gravity, or composing a haiku—the billions of cells work as a unified team.

To understand, explain, and practice this amazing activity, experts analyze it into separate skills such as remembering, classifying, and imagining. We need to remember that in reality, the various thinking skills are closely interrelated. Their boundaries often blur. Thus, when one of the skills is being practiced, almost certainly others are simultaneously being used. The following definitions of the thought processes focused on in this book show the integrated nature of thinking.

Analyzing: identifying the parts that make up a whole; taking something apart physically or conceptually. This activity is often an early step in problem solving, troubleshooting, and sequencing.

Brainstorming: listing elements, options, ideas, memories, possibilities, or variations without restraint. This "wild card" skill comes into play in many critical and creative thinking activities.

Changing point of view: observing or conceiving something from a new perspective. This could involve physically moving to a different position, for example, getting down on one's hands and knees to see what a baby sees. Or it could involve using the imagination to "think" like a one-celled animal.

Classifying: placing something into a group of related things for the sake of organizing or understanding. Classifying may involve comparing and contrasting, ordering, and labeling.

Comparing and contrasting: listing the ways two or more things are alike and different. This process may involve the use of diagrams for processing data.

Deductive reasoning: drawing one or more conclusions from available information.

Defining concepts: stating the relationship between a thing and a class of things to which it belongs. The task involves analyzing, comparing and contrasting. Defining can play a key role in explaining a thing or concept.

Evaluating: using criteria to determine the worth or quality of a thing. Evaluating is often a component of problem solving because the problem solver must often choose the "best" solution from several possibilities.

Experimenting: making observations under controlled (artificial) circumstances to discover a fact or to evaluate the validity of an assertion.

Finding patterns: identifying a recurring sequence of things in a set, for example, the fact that city names begin with a capital letter. Finding patterns involves observing and remembering (or note taking).

Formulating questions: stating an area of ignorance or uncertainty. On the surface, this would seem to be so simple an activity as to require no mental effort. But more than two thousand years ago Plato argued that the ability to ask questions may be the most difficult—and important—thinking process.

Generalizing: identifying attributes shared by all members of a set by studying a sampling. Generalizing typically involves observing or experimenting.

Hypothesizing: guessing at the explanation of a mystery. The activity often leads to experimenting.

Imagining: mentally picturing a thing or event, often for the purpose of predicting or problem solving.

Inventing: creating a thing or process that is different in one or more ways from an existing thing or process. This task often involves synthesizing because most inventions blend elements of earlier inventions. Successful inventing also may require problem solving, visual thinking, and evaluating.

Observing: gaining information through purposeful perception. Observing suggests active—rather than passive—use of one or more of the five senses. Observers typically know what they are looking for. This process is a major part of experimenting.

Ordering: arranging items of a set according to articulated criteria, for example, "largest to smallest" or "first to last" or "most efficient to least efficient."

Predicting: describing something that does not exist but that one expects will exist in the future. Predicting is an important part of experimenting. After making a prediction, the experimenter sets up a situation in which the expected event is looked for.

Problem solving: devising a plan to overcome an obstacle. This activity generally involves analyzing or defining concepts (to determine the specific problem), brainstorming (to generate competing solutions), and evaluating (to find the best solution according to criteria such as cost or ease).

Remembering: bringing stored information into consciousness. Remembering makes possible many other mental tasks, including finding patterns and problem solving.

Summarizing: abstracting the most important ideas or facts from a statement, report, or other work. The activity often involves translating.

Synthesizing: bringing together two or more things or processes to invent a new thing or process. For example, the airplane was a synthesis of the glider, the ship's propeller, and the gasoline engine.

Translating: changing the form of a message from one medium or language to another. Writing a French story in English is translating; so is turning a novel into a movie script or a poem into a short story.

Troubleshooting: reviewing and then revising procedures in order to change an unfavorable outcome into a desirable one. This may involve observing, analyzing, comparing and contrasting, hypothesizing, problem solving, experimenting, and evaluating.

Visual thinking: translating ideas into mental or actual images, for example, making a pictorial representation of a verbal math problem.

Inventors' Workshop

In the nineteenth century, the head of the U.S. Patent Office wrote to Congress that he believed most of the useful inventions had already been invented!

Fortunately, hundreds and thousands of inventive people didn't get that bureaucrat's message. They were too busy puzzling and tinkering and designing and experimenting. Thanks to them, today we have everything from computers and CDs to Velcro and VCRs.

But is there anything left to invent? As long as we nurture the imagination of our young people and teach them the methods of innovation, the answer will be a great big YES.

Here are suggestions for a three-stage class project to help your students tap their creativity, use critical thinking, and share the joy of inventing.

1. Teach the heritage of invention.

As with most human activities, with inventing it's often "Monkey see, monkey do." To put it more positively, students need to hear about inventors and their work.

- Read about inventors and inventions. You'll find a few relevant books in the reading list, but your school and local libraries are sure to have dozens more. Read to the students, have them read to each other, and encourage independent reading as well.
- Write to companies that market patented products and ask for behind-the-scenes information on how the products were developed. Try toy companies, hardware companies, household product companies. The mailing address is usually printed on the box.
- Invite local inventors to visit your classroom and talk about their work. To find them, contact your newspaper or your college or university. Ask the guests to bring prototypes, drawings, and patent documents. (If you find out the number of any patent, you can receive a copy of the actual patent by sending $1.50 to the Patent and Trademark Office, Washington, D.C. 20231.)
- Maintain an ongoing "Invention Bulletin Board." Fill it with stories from local newspapers and science

magazines. Many papers carry a syndicated, once-a-week invention column called "Patent File: The Latest in New Ideas and Inventions" by Edmund Andrews of *The New York Times*.

When working with younger children, you could simply read aloud news of recent inventions.

2. Teach students to be aware of problems.

Inventors often swing into action when they notice something that "isn't quite right" or "could be better."

- Have students keep inventors' notebooks in which they write about problems. (Instead of keeping separate notebooks, students could devote a section of their regular notebooks to invention.)
- Have students ask their parents to suggest problems around the house that need to be dealt with.
- Regularly study familiar objects with the aim of coming up with improvements. (The majority of inventions are actually improvements of earlier inventions, for example, "a bath soap that floats.")
- Maintain a bulletin board with a title like "There ought to be a ..." or "I wish there were a ..."

3. Sponsor an invention fair.

Have students, working alone or in small groups, dream up novelties that are, in theory at least, practical given current knowledge. This means that time machines are probably off-limits, whereas a "floating soap dish" might make sense.

Students should prepare diagrams and sketches of their inventions, along with text that explains what the inventions will do. In some cases, they might be able to make working models called "prototypes."

Set aside time for students to present their inventions to their classmates and to other students throughout the school. Encourage students to make a display, use the overhead projector, and practice good speech-making skills during their presentations. You might also include news of these inventions in your home-school flyer and invite parents to view the items at your inventions fair.

Wise Words

The following quotations shed light on many facets of thinking. You might use these observations in your home-school newsletter or at open-house meetings.

ART
People paint with their brains, not with their hands.
—Michelangelo

CURIOSITY
Curiosity is one of the permanent and certain characteristics of a vigorous intellect.
—Dr. Johnson

DISCOVERY
We can learn something new any time we believe we can.
—Virginia Satir

From the very beginning of his education, the child should experience the joy of discovery.
—Alfred North Whitehead

EXPERIMENT
It often happens that an unsuccessful experiment may produce an excellent observation. There are, therefore, no unsuccessful experiments.
—Claude Bernard

IMAGINATION
Imagination is more important than knowledge.
—Albert Einstein

KNOWLEDGE
Not to know is bad; not to wish to know is worse.
—African proverb

MEMORY
Memory is the art of attention.
—Dr. Johnson

OBSERVING
All our knowledge has its origins in our perceptions.
—Leonardo da Vinci

Is ditch water dull? Naturalists with microscopes have told me that it teems with quiet fun.
—G.K. Chesterton

PATTERNS

A mathematician, like a painter or a poet, is a maker of patterns.

—G.H. Hardy

POINT OF VIEW

You come to know a thing by being inside it.

—Edmund Carpenter

He who knows only his own side of the case knows little of that.

—John Stuart Mill

PROBLEM SOLVING

A problem well stated is a problem half solved.

—Charles Kettering

A good problem statement often includes (a) what is known, (b) what is unknown, and (c) what is sought.

—Edward Hodnett

QUESTIONS

If we would have new knowledge, we must get a whole world of new questions.

—Susan Langer

Judge people by their questions rather than by their answers.

—Voltaire

THINKING FOR YOURSELF

Thinking is like living and dying; you must do it for yourself.

—Anonymous

WISDOM

The door to wisdom swings on hinges of common sense and uncommon thoughts.

—Anonymous

WONDER

Wonder implies the desire to learn.

—Aristotle

Children's Books and Thinking Skills

Here is a sampler of books that celebrate all sorts of brain work. Reading one of these short picture books aloud may be the perfect way to introduce an activity.

COMPARING AND CONTRASTING
Karen's Opposites by Alice Provensen (Golden Press, 1963)
Opposites by Carol Watson (Usborne, 1983)
What the Moon Saw by Brian Wildsmith (Oxford University Press, 1978)

DEDUCTIVE REASONING
If I Had a Birthday Every Day by C. H. Gervais (Black Mountain/Firefly, 1983)
If You Give a Mouse a Cookie by Laura Numeroff (Harper and Row, 1985)

DEFINING CONCEPTS
A Snake Is Totally Tail by Judi Barrett (Macmillan, 1987)

HYPOTHESIZING
Hunches in Bunches by Dr. Seuss (Random House, 1982)
Yellow & Pink by William Steig (Farrar, 1984)

IMAGINING
Cloudy with a Chance of Meatballs by Judi Barrett (Atheneum, 1980)
Come Away from the Water, Shirley by John Burningham (Crowell, 1977)
How Georgina Drove the Car Very Carefully from Boston to New York by Lucy Bate (Crown, 1989)
Maggie B by Irene Haas (Atheneum, 1975)

INVENTING
Inventors Workshop by Alan McCormack (Fearon, 1981)
Steven Caney's Invention Book by Steven Caney (Workman, 1985)
Why Didn't I Think of That? From Alarm Clocks to Zippers by Webb Garrison (Prentice-Hall, 1977)

OBSERVING
Blind Men and the Elephant by Lillian Fox Quigley (Scribner, 1959)
I See by Rachel Isadora (Greenwillow, 1985)
Look Again by Tona Hoban (Macmillan, 1971)
Look Closer! by Peter Zeibel (Clarion, 1989)

One Day I Closed My Eyes and the World Disappeared
by Elizabeth Bram (Dial, 1978)

Small Worlds Close Up by Lisa Grillone and Joseph
Genaro (Crown, 1978)

Smallest Life Around Us by Lucia Anderson (Crown, 1978)

We Hide, You Seek by Jose Aruego and Ariane Dewey
(Greenwillow, 1979)

PICTOGRAPHS/REBUSES

Bunny Rabbit Rebus by David Adler (Crowell, 1983)

Mother Goose in Hieroglyphics by George Appleton
(Houghton Mifflin, 1962)

Rebus Treasury by Jean Marzollo (Dial, 1986)

POINT OF VIEW

Big World, Small World by Jeanne Titherington
(Greenwillow, 1985)

From Where You Are by Joyce Wakefield (Children's
Press, 1978)

Three D, Two D, One D by David Adler (Crowell, 1975)

PROBLEM SOLVING

Albert's Alphabet by Leslie Tryon (Atheneum, 1991)

Charlie Needs a Cloak by Tomie de Paola (Prentice-
Hall, 1973)

Detective of London by Robert Kraus (Dutton, 1978)

It Could Always Be Worse by Margot Zemach (Farrar, 1976)

Mouse Soup by Arnold Lobel (Harper, 1977)

Runaway Bunny by Margaret Wise Brown (Harper, 1942)

We're in Big Trouble, Blackboard Bear by Martha
Alexander (Dial, 1980)

QUESTIONING

How Come Elephants? by Mark Simont (Harper, 1965)

If He's My Brother by Barbara Williams (Harvey House, 1976)

May I Stay? by Harry Allard (Prentice-Hall, 1977)

Owley by Mike Thaler (Harper, 1982)

Wait Till the Moon Is Full by Margaret Wise Brown
(Harper, 1948)

When? What? Why? Where? How? Who? by Jane Belk
Moncure (Children's Press, 1984)

SIMILES

As: A Surfeit of Similes by Norton Juster (Morrow, 1989)

Easy as Pie by Marcia and Michael Folsom (Clarion, 1985)

INDEX

Words and phrases that appear in all capital letters are activity names.
The activities are presented in alphabetical order starting on page 7.